WITHDRAWN

Sports Illustrated KIDS

STARS OF SPORTS

LAMAR JACKSON

SUPERSTAR QUARTERBACK

■■■ by Matt Chandler

CAPSTONE PRESS
a capstone imprint

Stars of Sports is published by
Capstone Press, an imprint of Capstone
1710 Roe Crest Drive, North Mankato, Minnesota 56003
www.capstonepub.com

Library of Congress Cataloging-in-Publication Data
Names: Chandler, Matt, author.
Title: Lamar Jackson : superstar quarterback / Matt Chandler.
Description: North Mankato, Minnesota : Capstone Press, [2021] |
Series: SIK stars of sports | Includes bibliographical references and index. |
Audience: Ages 8-11 | Audience: Grades 4-6 |
Summary: "Quarterback Lamar Jackson became the NFL's Most Valuable Player in 2019. It was only his second year in the league. Readers will learn how Jackson overcame a difficult childhood and went on to become one of the NFL's rising stars and the youngest quarterback to ever start in a playoff game!"—Provided by publisher.
Identifiers: LCCN 2021006169 (print) | LCCN 2021006170 (ebook) |
ISBN 9781663907233 (Hardcover) | ISBN 9781663907202 (PDF) |
ISBN 9781663907226 (Kindle Edition)
Subjects: LCSH: Jackson, Lamar, 1997- | Football players—United States—Biography—Juvenile literature. | Quarterbacks (Football)—United States—Biography—Juvenile literature.
Classification: LCC GV939.J29 C43 2021 (print) | LCC GV939.J29 (ebook) |
DDC 796.332092 [B]—dc23
LC record available at https://lccn.loc.gov/2021006169
LC ebook record available at https://lccn.loc.gov/2021006170

Editorial Credits
Editor: Mandy Robbins; Designer: Dina Her; Media Researcher: Morgan Walters; Production Specialist: Tori Abraham

Image Credits
Associated Press: David Blair/Icon Sportswire, 5, Gail Burton, 21, Ian Johnson/Icon Sportswire, 17, Joy Asico, 28, Julio Cortez, 22, Nick Wass, 18, Perry Knotts, 23; Newscom: Allen Eyestone/ZUMA Press, 11, Andy Lewis/Icon Sportswire, Cover, Damon Higgins/ZUMA Press, 8, David Tulis/UPI, 24, John Angelillo/UPI, 7, Rich Graessle/Icon Sportswire, 15, Stephen Furst/Icon Sportswire, 12; Shutterstock: Alex Kravtsov, 1; Sports Illustrated: Erick W. Rasco, 27

TABLE OF CONTENTS

RECORD BREAKER 4

CHAPTER ONE
GROWING UP IN FLORIDA 6

CHAPTER TWO
COLLEGE BOUND 10

CHAPTER THREE
WELCOME TO THE NFL! 16

CHAPTER FOUR
MVP SEASON 20

CHAPTER FIVE
THE FUTURE LOOKS BRIGHT 26

TIMELINE 29
GLOSSARY 30
READ MORE 31
INTERNET SITES 31
INDEX...32

Words in **BOLD** are in the glossary.

RECORD BREAKER

Lamar Jackson played 38 college games at the University of Louisville in Kentucky. In 37 of those games, he was a very good quarterback. But on September 1, 2016, he was unstoppable.

Jackson's Louisville Cardinals were playing the University of North Carolina-Charlotte 49ers. Three minutes into the game, Jackson broke two tackles. He raced for a 36-yard (33-meter) touchdown. But he didn't stop there. By the time the first half was over, he had set a school record. Jackson scored eight touchdowns! He threw for six and ran for two. Thanks to his awesome play, Louisville led 56–0 at halftime.

At that point, his coach took Jackson out of the game. Jackson's eight touchdowns in a half were the most in the history of Louisville football.

>>> Jackson throws a pass during his record-setting game on September 1, 2016.

FACT

When a team has a big lead, coaches often take out their best players. That gives other players a chance to play and keeps the starting players from getting injured.

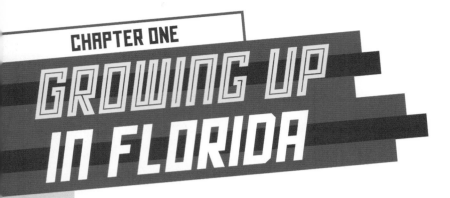

CHAPTER ONE

GROWING UP IN FLORIDA

Jackson was born in Pompano Beach, Florida, on January 7, 1997. When he was eight years old, his dad died. Jackson's mom, Felicia Jones, raised Jackson and his younger brother, Jamar. Jackson has said when his dad died, he became a "mama's boy."

It was his mom who helped make him a great football player. She trained with him every day. She made him run across a bridge near his home to build up his speed. She bought him football pads. She ran drills with him in the backyard of their home. Jackson has called her the best coach he ever had.

"She had a vision for my football career even before I did," he wrote in *The Player's Tribune* in 2016.

〉〉〉 Jackson and his mom after his Heisman Trophy win

Early Training

Jackson's mom wanted him to be the best. When he was eight, she got him his own private coach, Van Warren. Warren would work with Jackson every Sunday. He pushed the young boy through hours of football drills in the Florida heat.

"I used to complain a lot," Jackson said. "There were days I was like, 'Mom, I don't want to go today.'" That early training helped prepare him for life as an NFL superstar.

7

〉〉〉 Jackson scrambles to avoid being tackled.

FACT

Growing up in Florida, Jackson played youth football in a league with Marquise Brown. The two men are now teammates as members of the Baltimore Ravens.

HIGH SCHOOL BALLER

Jackson began his high school football career at Santaluces Community High School. For his junior year, he moved to Boynton Beach High School. His mom felt it would give Jackson the best chance to succeed.

Jackson played the quarterback position at Boynton Beach. As a junior, he tossed 19 touchdown passes. He ran for 10 more.

His best high school game came in his senior season. Boynton Beach was taking on Village Academy. Jackson tossed a long touchdown and ran for two more scores. It was his second rushing TD that made Jackson go **viral**. First he escaped pressure by the defense. Then he ran to the right and raced 25 yards (23 m) toward the end zone. As a Village Academy defender closed in for the hit, Jackson slammed on the brakes. The defender ran past him and Jackson walked into the end zone! His team won the game 50–8.

CHAPTER TWO

COLLEGE BOUND

College scouts followed Jackson's high school games closely. Major college football programs **recruited** him. The Clemson Tigers, Florida State Seminoles, Louisville Cardinals, and South Carolina Gamecocks all offered Jackson **scholarships**.

Jackson's mom was helping guide his decision. Many teams recruiting Jackson wanted to make him a wide receiver. They thought his speed would make Jackson impossible to cover. His mom didn't want Jackson to play wide receiver. She knew her son had the talent to be a superstar at quarterback.

She talked with Louisville coach Bobby Petrino. He promised her that Jackson could be a quarterback for the Cardinals. Petrino was known for training great quarterbacks. Jackson and his mom chose the Louisville Cardinals.

〉〉〉 Jackson announced that he signed with the Louisville Cardinals on February 4, 2015.

>>> Jackson runs for a touchdown during the Music City Bowl, December 30, 2015.

Speedy Quarterback

Jackson was so fast, his coaches at Louisville wanted him to play other positions. But Head Coach Bobby Petrino had promised Jackson's mom her son would only play quarterback. They simply couldn't use his speed at other positions. So, the Louisville coaches built a playbook around Jackson running the ball. In his three seasons there, Jackson ran the ball 655 times. He rushed for more than 4,000 yards (3,658 m). He even ran for 50 touchdowns!

YOUNG CARDINAL

Jackson began his college career as the backup quarterback to starter Reggie Bonnafon. In his first game, the Cardinals ran a trick play with both quarterbacks on the field. Jackson took the ball and threw his first college pass down the field. It was a terrible throw. It was easily **intercepted** by Auburn's Tray Matthews. Auburn beat Louisville 31–24.

Luckily for Jackson, things got better. His best game of the season came in a win against Texas A&M in the Music City Bowl. Late in the first quarter, Jackson ran up the middle. He sped past tacklers. Then Jackson raced down the field 61 yards (56 m) for the touchdown! He passed for two touchdowns and ran for two. Jackson led the Cardinals to a 27–21 win.

HEISMAN HERO

Jackson began his second college season as the team's starting quarterback. He won his first four games.

Jackson finished the season averaging more than 100 rushing yards (91.5 m) per game. But he wanted to prove he was more than just fast. He wanted to prove he could throw the ball like a star. He did that in his second season in Louisville. In one game, Jackson threw for 417 yards (381 m). He added five touchdowns. He threw for more than 300 yards (274 m) four times in 2016.

Jackson beat teams with his passing. He beat teams with his running. He led the Cardinals to a record of 9–4. Jackson became the youngest player ever to win the **Heisman Trophy.**

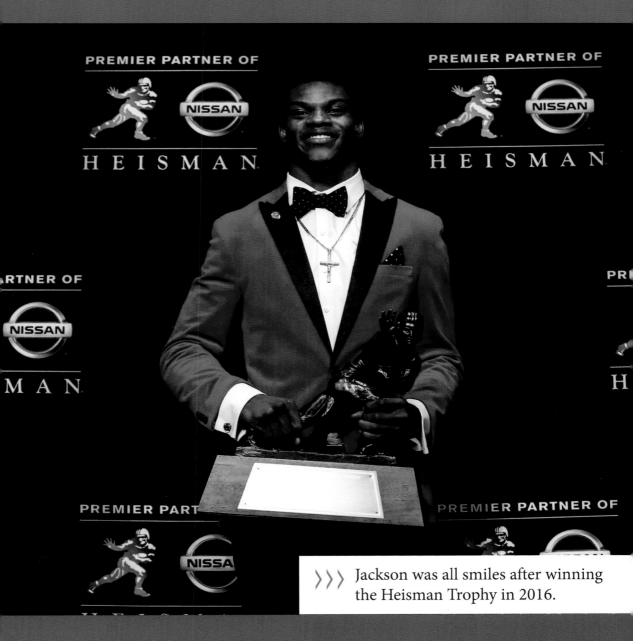

>>> Jackson was all smiles after winning the Heisman Trophy in 2016.

CHAPTER THREE

WELCOME TO THE NFL!

Most football experts expected Jackson to leave college early and enter the **NFL Draft**. He was expected to be a first-round draft pick. One bad game may have helped make that decision easier. It came on September 16, 2017. The Cardinals took on their **rival**, the Clemson Tigers. Clemson easily beat them 47–21. The low point for Jackson came when Clemson's Dorian O'Daniel leaped and picked off Jackson. He raced 44 yards (40 m) for the touchdown. Jackson was also **sacked** four times in the game.

The loss made Jackson realize that if he kept playing poorly or got hurt, he could lose NFL Draft value. Jackson didn't want to risk that. At the end of the season, he announced on Twitter that he was leaving Louisville for the NFL.

"After much discussion with my family and coaches, I have made the decision to take the next step in my career and enter the 2018 NFL Draft," Jackson wrote.

〉〉〉 Jackson carried the ball downfield for the Cardinals during a 2017 game against the Clemson Tigers.

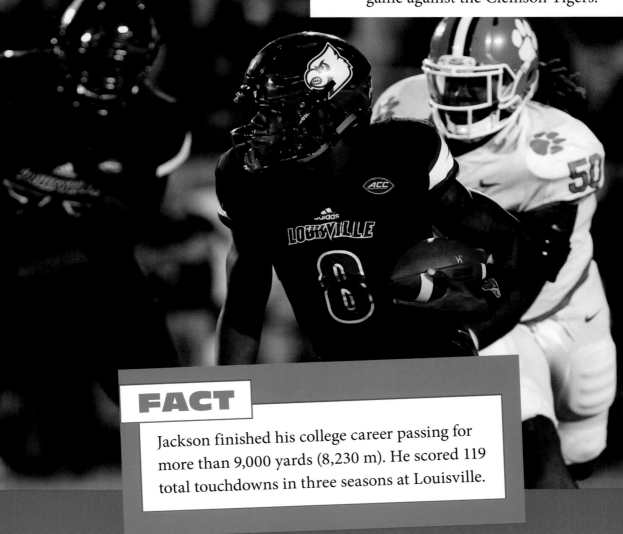

FACT

Jackson finished his college career passing for more than 9,000 yards (8,230 m). He scored 119 total touchdowns in three seasons at Louisville.

》》》 Jackson fights off a tackle by Bengals cornerback Darqueze Dennard.

Jackson was one of several talented quarterbacks in the 2018 NFL Draft. His passing game wasn't as strong as the other quarterbacks. Some people said that would keep teams from picking him early in the draft. The other four quarterbacks were all chosen early in the draft. The Baltimore Ravens used the final pick of the first round to choose Jackson.

Jackson started his first NFL game in Week 11 against the Cincinnati Bengals. Starter Joe Flacco injured his hip against the Pittsburgh Steelers and couldn't play.

Jackson was nervous to be making his first start. "I had butterflies before the first tackle," he said, "But after the first tackle, it was game on."

Jackson rushed for 117 yards (107 m). He led his team to a 24–21 win. He finished his **rookie** season with just one loss as a starter and led his team to the playoffs.

CHAPTER FOUR

MVP SEASON

After Jackson's strong first season, the Ravens traded Joe Flacco. Jackson was now their starting quarterback. One month into the season, Jackson had lost two games. Had the Ravens made the wrong decision? Jackson answered that question by winning his next 11 starts!

His biggest game of 2019 came in his final regular season start. Jackson led the Ravens to a 31–15 win over the Cleveland Browns. Jackson threw three touchdowns. The biggest one was a 39-yard (36-m) touchdown pass to Mark Andrews. It gave the Ravens their first lead of the game. Jackson led his team to the playoffs in his first two seasons in the league!

>>> Mark Andrews catches Jackson's 39-yard (36-m) touchdown pass.

The Ravens were a favorite to win the Super Bowl as the playoffs began. But they disappointed their fans. On January 11, 2020, Jackson led his team against the Tennessee Titans. More than 71,000 Ravens fans packed M&T Bank Stadium to watch their young superstar. For the second season, Jackson didn't deliver a playoff win. The Titans sacked Jackson four times and intercepted him twice. They easily beat the Ravens 28–12.

〉〉〉 Jackson slipped out of a tackle during the game against the Titans.

Jackson had some advice for other players after the game. "Don't underestimate your opponents," he said. "They caught us (by) surprise. That's all it was."

Even though they lost, Jackson finished the season with 3,127 yards (2,835 m) passing, 1,206 yards (1,103 m) rushing, and 43 total touchdowns. Those numbers earned him the league MVP Award.

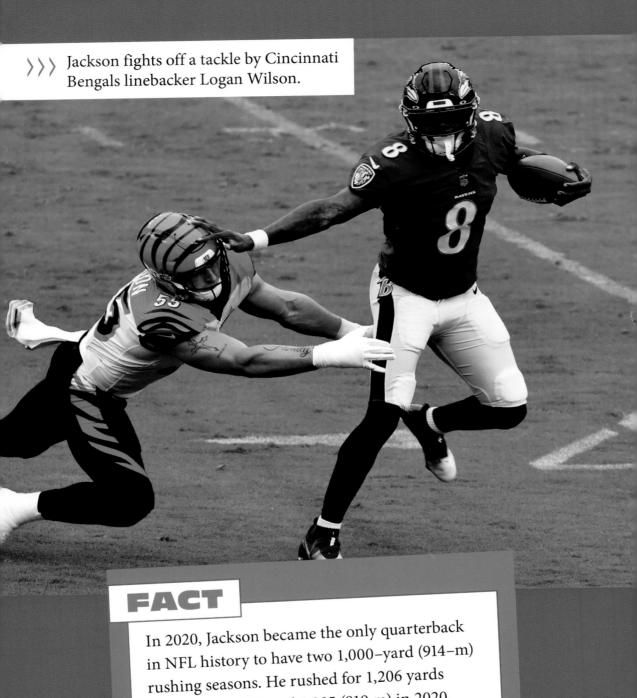

›› ›
Jackson fights off a tackle by Cincinnati Bengals linebacker Logan Wilson.

FACT

In 2020, Jackson became the only quarterback in NFL history to have two 1,000–yard (914–m) rushing seasons. He rushed for 1,206 yards (1,103 m) in 2019 and 1,005 (919 m) in 2020.

PANDEMIC PLAY

Jackson led his team to a 5–1 start in 2020. It was a tough year, playing during the **COVID-19 pandemic**. But could this be the year he led his team to the Super Bowl? After an up-and-down season, the Ravens finished the season 11–5. It was good enough to earn a Wild-Card spot in the playoffs.

The Ravens faced the Buffalo Bills in the second round of the playoffs. Jackson had one of his worst games of the season. The low point came when he threw an interception. It was returned for a 101-yard (92-meter) touchdown—a playoff record. Jackson's season ended when he was knocked out of the game with a concussion. Once again, he came up short in his attempt to lead the Ravens to the Super Bowl.

CHAPTER FIVE

THE FUTURE LOOKS BRIGHT

Quarterbacks that run a lot have a better chance of getting injured. Jackson rushed more than 450 times in three seasons. Michael Vick, Cam Newton and Steve Young were known as running quarterbacks. Each suffered serious injuries that hurt their careers.

Running quarterbacks aren't usually as successful in the NFL for a long period of time. Even though he is one of the best running QBs in the NFL, Jackson wants to be known as a passer. "I hate running," Jackson said in 2019. "I'll do it, but I'd rather just sit back and pass it. I like throwing touchdowns instead of running them."

〉〉〉 Jackson slips out of Wesley Woodward's grasp as he rushes down the field.

FACT

Jackson's 1,206 (1,103 m) rushing yards in 2019 was sixth most in the NFL. He even beat out the starting running backs for 27 NFL teams!

PLAYOFF POWER

Jackson is one of the most exciting players to watch in the NFL. He can beat teams with his arm. He can beat teams with his legs. But so far, he hasn't found success in the playoffs.

In his first three seasons, the Ravens were 1–3 in the postseason. Jackson completed just 55 percent of his playoff passes. He threw four interceptions in the three losses.

His fans want Jackson to take the Ravens to the Super Bowl. Only time will tell if that will happen.

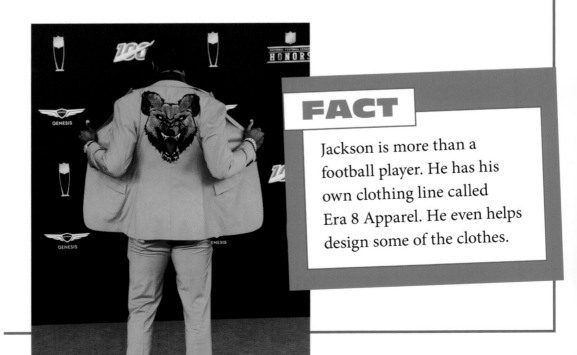

FACT

Jackson is more than a football player. He has his own clothing line called Era 8 Apparel. He even helps design some of the clothes.

TIMELINE

1997 Jackson is born in Pompano Beach, Florida, on January 7.

2013 Jackson transfers to Boynton Beach High School for his junior year.

2014 Jackson commits to attend college at the University of Louisville.

2015 Jackson is named MVP of the Music City Bowl.

2016 Jackson wins the Heisman Trophy as college football's top player.

2018 Jackson announces he will skip his senior year to enter the NFL Draft.

2018 He is selected by the Baltimore Ravens with the 32nd pick in the NFL Draft.

2019 Jackson sets an NFL record as the youngest quarterback to ever start a playoff game.

2019 Jackson wins the NFL MVP Award.

2020 He is named the starting quarterback of the Pro Bowl.

GLOSSARY

COVID-19 PANDEMIC (KOH-vid-nine-TEEN pan-DEH-mik)—a very contagious and sometimes deadly virus that spread worldwide in 2020

HEISMAN TROPHY (HISE-muhn TROH-fee)—an award given each year to the best college football player in America

INTERCEPT (in-tur-SEPT)—to catch a pass made by an opposing player

NFL DRAFT (EN-eff-el DRAFT)—an event in which athletes are picked to join teams in the National Football League

RECRUIT (ri-KROOT)—to ask someone to join a college team

RIVAL (RYE-vuhl)—someone whom a person competes against

ROOKIE (RUK-ee)—a first-year player

SACK (SAK)—when a defensive player tackles the opposing quarterback behind the line of scrimmage

SCHOLARSHIP (SKOL-ur-ship)—money given to a student to pay for school

UNANIMOUS (yoo-NAN-uh-muhss)—agreed on by everyone

VIRAL (VYE-ruhl)—becoming very popular by circulating quickly from person to person, especially through the internet

READ MORE

Aretha, David. *Top 10 Craziest Plays in Football.* New York: Enslow Publishing, LLC, 2017.

Chandler, Matt. *Patrick Mahomes: Football MVP.* North Mankato, MN: Capstone Press, 2020.

Jankowski, Matt. *The Greatest Football Players of All Time.* New York: Gareth Stevens Publishing, 2020.

INTERNET SITES

Lamar Jackson
espn.com/nfl/player/_/id/3916387

Pro Football Reference Stats Page
pro-football-reference.com/players/J/JackLa00.htm

Ravens Team Bio
baltimoreravens.com/team/players-roster/lamar-jackson/

INDEX

Andrews, Mark, 20, 21

Baltimore Ravens, 8, 19, 20, 22, 25, 28

Boynton Beach High School, 9

college career, 4, 10, 13, 14, 16, 17

Era 8 Apparel, 28

Flacco, Joe, 19, 20

Heisman Trophy, 7, 14, 15

Jones, Felicia, 6, 7, 9, 10, 12

Louisville Cardinals, 4, 10, 11, 12, 13, 14, 16, 17

NFL Draft, 16–17, 19

Petrino, Bobby, 10, 12

records, 4, 5, 14, 25

Santaluces Community High School, 9

Warren, Van, 7